Couponing for the Everyday Consumer

It's not just about extreme couponing!

By
Jenn Greenleaf

All rights reserved. Published by Jenn Greenleaf in the United States of America.
© March 2013 by Jenn Greenleaf

ISBN-13: 978-1482773798
ISBN-10: 1482773791

Cover Design by Jenn Greenleaf. Image courtesy of Jenn Greenleaf's Flickr.com album.

Interior photography courtesy of Jenn Greenleaf's Flickr.com album and Stock Exchange.

Table of Contents

Introduction: 4

    We all have to begin somewhere! 4

Chapter One: 8

    How We Handle Christmas and Birthday Gifts 8

Chapter 2: 14

    Why My Husband Won't Grocery Shop 14

Chapter 3: 20

    How Else Can I Save Money on Groceries? 20

Chapter four: 25

    What the Heck Are You Talking About? 25

Chapter Five: 28

    Couponing Organizing Tips 28

Chapter Six: 32

    Wait. What About Rain Checks & Rebates? 32

Chapter Seven: 36

    Knowledge is Power! 36

    Create a Household Binder 36

Chapter Seven: 41
   What is the Purpose of a Stockpile? 41

Chapter Eight: 45
   How Else Can We Save More Money? 45

Conclusion 50
   Are You Ready to Start Saving? 50

Resources: 53
   Resource Links I've Used Along the Way 53

Appendix A: 54
   Shopping List 54

Appendix B: 55
   Price Tracking Chart 55

Appendix C: 56
   Meal Planner 56

Appendix D: 57
   Pantry Inventory 57

Appendix E: 58
   Freezer Inventory 58

About the Author 59

Introduction:

We all have to begin somewhere!

"Never spend your money before you have it."

-Thomas Jefferson

These are the notes I take during ad match-up's.

Everyone has their own reasons for why they want to save money using coupons.

- Are you tired of paying full price for groceries, toiletries, and health and beauty items?

- Would you like to find ways to save money on other household items, home improvement products, and clothing?

- Do you have a large family you're trying to stretch dollars as far as possible for?

- Are you a student working with a small budget?

As you can see if you answered yes to any of the questions above, there are people from all walks of life and all financial situations benefit from couponing. Because prices in the consumer marketplace continue to rise, it's time to think creatively about how we're spending our hard earned dollars. Using coupons is not a new concept, however many of the strategies associated with the term "couponing" are.

My story is similar to many others seeking new and innovative ways to save money. My husband and I are both self-employed (he's a building contractor and I'm a freelance writer), so our income is unpredictable. This makes it difficult to develop a steady budget, so this is a task I have to tackle on a weekly basis. The first thing I realized is we have a lot of controls over many of our expenditures, including groceries and other household necessities.

For example, my husband has a twelve year old daughter and I have two sons that are eleven and thirteen. When we blended our family together the kids were two, three, and four. My youngest was still in diapers until he turned three so, in the lifetime of our relationship so far, we've gone from finding good deals on diapers to finding good deals on electronics. It's amazing how quickly the kids have grown and, along the way, how much their needs have changed.

The first thing we did was set up a budget for Christmas and birthdays. As difficult as it is, we stick to this budget every year. We send $100 per child for Christmas gifts and we spend $50 per child for their birthdays. We have this same budget for when we buy birthday and anniversary gifts for each other, as well. This budget has worked for us up until this past year because it was the first time the kids gave us lists containing expensive electronics and games on them. That doesn't mean the kids had a disappointing Christmas or birthday, though. This means it was time for me to think even MORE creatively about how to make these things happen.

Chapter One:

How We Handle Christmas and Birthday Gifts

"People first, then money, then things."

- Suze Orman

My oldest son's lobster boat is a work in progress.

When it comes to saving and stretching money, I'm considered an unconventional thinker. We live in a society where children seem entitled to receive this, that, or the other thing. So, when our children ask us for large ticket items when it isn't Christmas or birthday season, we tell them they need to work to earn the money. For example, my oldest son mowed lawns last summer and saved throughout the season so he could buy a used lobster boat and some traps. Then, he pooled the rest of his money together from his birthday and his other odd jobs to buy and used iPod Touch from Amazon.com. He still has over $200 in the bank to use toward fixing up his boat and other items he'll need when he starts lobstering next year.

Because he was twelve years old when he did this, some people balked at the notion that he had to work so hard to earn those things. In my opinion, teaching the kids to do these things while they're still young helps them understand how expensive everything is and how hard everyone has to work for what they want. This leads me to how we handle expensive birthday and Christmas gifts. We approach this in a couple of different ways:

A. **Scenario #1:** we know what each member of our family has budgeted for Christmas and birthday gifts so, if the items fall in line with what they are spending alongside with our budget, we'll ask them to go in with us on a combined gift. For example, my youngest son wanted an X-Box 360 for his birthday. That, of course, exceeded our $50 budget, so I thought creatively. We were able to go in with three other family members so he could get the console, an extra controller, and a game.

B. **Scenario #2:** when the kids ask for a gift that exceeds our budget and other family members choose not to do a combined gift with us, we'll give the kids money in a card to go toward the purchase they wanted to receive as a gift. Then, we'll give them opportunities to work off the remaining money they need. Sometimes they'll receive $5 or $10 in a card from other people at their birthday party or in Christmas cards, so they can use that to help save up for their purchase. For example, there were some Lego sets my stepdaughter wanted, so she was able to add up the money she received in cards and work off the rest.

The first time I explained these scenarios, the responses were interesting. "You don't give your kids Christmas or birthday presents?" "You make your kids work for their gifts?" "That's not fair; they should be getting what their friends are getting!" Okay, as you can see some of the responses were a bit heated. We do give our kids gifts, but we do not agree with spending $1,000's of dollars every (when you add up three kids for Christmas and three birthdays . . . it's a LOT of money) year. If they want these high ticket items, they have to earn them.

* * * * *

How do I stretch those budgets?

Even though our budgets are low, I have found ways to stretch those dollars until they scream. I already know I'm going to spend $50.00 or $100.00 depending on the occasion. So, out of that cash, I'll try to find coupons for stocking stuffers and I'll shop at the dollar store for other small items they always seem to run out of (cute erasers, neat pencils, paper, and art supplies). I'll also hit the clearance aisles throughout the year and stash those items in the back of my closet.

In addition to that, I use a large number of websites to earn Amazon.com gift cards. Some of my frequented sites include:

- **SwagBucks.com:** each time you earn 450 SwagBucks, you can cash them out for $5.00 Amazon.com gift cards. I start saving my "special occasion" gift cards around September or October. The rest of the year, I use the cards for toilet paper and other items I want to get for free. More on that later, though.

- **SocialMoms.com:** I'm new here, but I've seen other moms racking up the points toward Amazon.com gift cards, so I've added this to my list of active sites.

- **Bing.com Rewards:** this is another site I'm new at, but the points are adding up quickly. So, before long, I should be able to add these gift cards to the arsenal I've managed to wrangle up from SwagBucks.com.

- **MyPoints.com:** It takes me a little longer to earn Amazon.com gift cards using this site, but I may not be using it to its fullest benefit because I've read about how other bloggers are doing well on here.

Once I have all the gift cards earned, I divide them up by three. When shopping on Amazon.com, orders over $25.00 receive free shipping. So, I never have to worry about adding that into my budget. I just make sure I place my order by the first week of December for Christmas gifts and at least two weeks before birthdays so I have plenty of time to wrap. Most of the time, using the gift cards allows me to spend an additional $25.00 per child.

The kids know I do this and that's how my oldest son was able to get some extra money toward his iPod Touch and my stepdaughter was able to get some extra toward her Legos. So, the kids know I'm trying to be as creative with budgets as possible . . . and that there is no Santa.

If have more gift cards available, then I have more "free dollars" to spend . . . so, as you can see, our budget is merely a "this is all we will spend for cash out of pocket purchases." It's a little more work, but it's worth the effort when you're trying to control every penny being spent every year. (Even though it's impossible to track every penny – I can come close!)

Chapter 2:

Why My Husband Won't Grocery Shop . . .

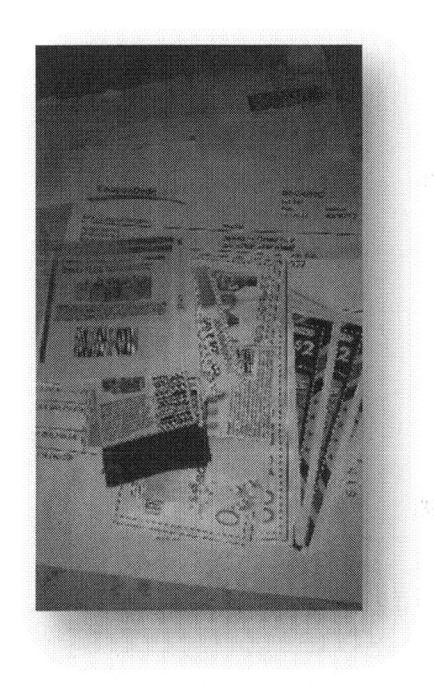

"Money often costs too much."

- Ralph Waldo Emerson

This trip was split into three different stores.

Okay, now we're going to get into grocery shopping. This is where I get to have fun shopping at a large number of stores (thankfully they are all in close proximity to each other) without spending a lot of money. My grocery budget is $75.00 per week, but I leave the store with a lot more product than that. My goal is to stretch our $300.00 monthly grocery bill to $1,000.00 without spending any extra money out of pocket (the abbreviation for out of pocket, by the way, is oop). This is a challenge and, at this point, I've only been able to stretch it to between $450.00 and $500.00. I'm working on this, though, and I'm confident I can achieve this goal.

How do I get started?

I spend between one and four hours per day couponing. I don't mean to sound harsh but, if an extreme couponer tells you they are spending less than one hour per day, they are not being honest with you. it takes time to find the deals, clip the coupons, organize everything, price match, and write out the grocery list. I'm trying to be as transparent and honest about the process as possible. It's not meant to discourage you, but rather to help you prepare your couponing schedule. If you want to make this work, you have to dedicate a chunk of time toward the effort. I spend the most time on Sundays because I receive my coupon orders (from http://www.couponsthingsbydede.com) on Friday and I buy two additional newspapers every Sunday. So, I'm clipping coupons and cleaning out my coupon binder on that day.

I use websites and blogs to find the majority of my deals. Then, once I'm finished perusing those resources, I go directly to the store's website to compare their sales flyer against the coupons I have. While the deal sites I use are comprehensive, there are some regional deals I could miss out on if I don't take this extra step. Here are the deal websites I frequent the most for my area (Maine):

1. **I Love to Gossip:** *Deals So Good You'll Want to Tell Your Friends*
http://www.ilovetogossip.com
The site owner, Chrystie, has expanded her

site to include deals by state and deals by store.

2. **The Thieving Bear:** *Couponing for the Real World*
   http://www.thethievingbear.com
   Even though this blogger is out of New Hampshire, I'm finding a LOT of deals that are in line with Maine stores.

3. **Maven of Savin':** *Savin' Money, Savin' Time . . . and saving my mind!*
   http://www.mavenofsavin.com
   I love the coupon match-up's, the online deals, and the freebies. The coupon database is a huge help, too!

4. **Sunday Coupon Preview:** *Don't Miss a Sunday Coupon!*
   http://www.sundaycouponpreview.com
   This site helps me decide how much to order from http://www.couponsthingsbydede.com and how many newspapers I want to buy (if any – some weeks I don't buy any at all).

I use these websites to help me develop shopping lists for the stores I frequent the most. Those stores include:

- **Shaw's Supermarket:** they double their coupons every day and have many web-exclusive deals in the way of printable coupons, adding coupons to their savings card, and more.

- **Wal-Mart:** they will price match, but some cashiers are not familiar with how to price match and use coupons. So, come prepared with the coupon policy and the sales flyers you'd like to ad match.

- **Rite-Aid Pharmacy:** they accept manufacturer coupons and offer what is called UP Rewards.

- **CVS Pharmacy:** there is a coupon machine located at the beginning of the store, so be sure to scan your card as soon as you get there to receive deals. They also accept manufacturer coupons and allow customers to earn Extra Bucks Rewards (EBRs).

- **The Dollar Tree:** as long as the items are not trial size, you can bring in a "$1.00 any" product coupon and only pay tax. For example, I had six coupons for $1.00 off shampoo. The shampoo was small, but it wasn't trial sized, so I was able to purchase all six for just tax.

- **Target:** there are many ways to save at this store including stacking their coupons with manufacturer coupons. In addition, some purchases allow customers to earn Target gift cards.

I don't shop at every single one of these stores every week, but I do hit at least three of them. The ones I visit the most are Wal-Mart and Shaw's. Due to the coupon policy at Shaw's, customers are only allowed to use four "like" coupons per transaction, so I often have between two and four transactions at a time. This is part of the reason why my husband will not go grocery shopping. First, he doesn't have the patience to match coupons with sales and second, he doesn't have the patience to separate transactions for the deepest discounts.

Chapter 3:

How Else Can I Save Money on Groceries?

"Money is only a tool. It will take you wherever you wish, but it will not replace you as the driver."

- Ayn Rand

Learn the tricks to shopping for FREE!

Okay, we've talked about using websites and price matching against sales. That's a great start – especially when you want to shop for FREE. Yes, you can get items for FREE. For example, Kozy Shack pudding cups are priced $1.00 each (everyday low price – not a sale), and I order $.50/1 coupons from http://www.couponsthingsbydede.com – these coupons double at my grocery store making each pudding cup free.

The first time I found something for free, I almost started dancing in the aisle. I usually can find shampoo, pasta, soup, sauce mixes, and frozen vegetables. There are many, many other deals out there, though.

In addition to using regular newspaper clipped coupons, I also use online printable coupons. I love it when I find coupons that have a double benefit like the ones on SwagBucks.com, for example. Each time a coupon is printed and redeemed from SwagBucks.com, the user is rewarded with 10 SwagBucks. If you use a lot of coupons like I do, this adds up quickly toward gift cards or whatever else you would like to redeem your SwagBucks earnings on. In addition to printing from SwagBucks.com, I also print form:

- **CouponNetwork:** *by Catalina*
  http://www.couponnetwork.com
  In addition to finding great coupons, there are YourBucks offers. This is when customers purchase a certain quantity of items and receive a Catalina coupon when their register receipt prints out. For example, I used the YourBucks offer to purchase Capri Sun juice pouches (two separate transactions, four packages in each transaction). I purchased four and received a $3.00 coupon for my next order. I used it for my next order which also earned me a $3.00 coupon. To top it off, the juices were on sale for 2/$3.00 and I had two "buy 3 get one free" coupons to use with each

transaction. This is a great example of using a sale, a coupon, and a YourBucks offer lumped together for a deep discount.

- **SmartSource.com:** *Online Coupons*
  http://smartsource.com/smartsource
  The coupons available here load on the first of each month and are similar to what is offered in the Sunday newspaper. This is a great opportunity when you find a stock up price on something. For example, salad dressing went on sale for $1.00 a piece and I found a $.55 coupon on here for it that will double at my grocery store. My grocery store does not pay overages (but Wal-Mart DOES – keep that in mind!). So, when the coupon doubles, it makes the item free.

- **RedPlum:** *Now Known as Save.com*
  http://www.save.com/coupons/
  This is another printable coupon site that is very much in line with what is available in the Sunday newspaper coupon inserts. The coupon prints run out quickly here, though, so you really have to stay on top of it if you want to get the best deals. There have been times I've followed a link from a blogger and the prints were all used up already. So, be prepared for that.

- **Facebook.com:** *Not just for socializing!*
  http://www.facebook.com
  There are a TON of products and manufacturers that use Facebook.com pages and feature coupons for users regularly.

Sometimes, like in the case of Pepsi Next, visitors are able to pick up coupons for free items. Sometimes the coupon prints right then and there, while other times you have to fill out a request for and it is mailed to you. These Facebook.com only offers are not typically found on the regular printable sites, so keep your eyes peeled!

- **Manufacturer Websites:** *Their Coupons and Promotions Links*
  There are over 1,000 websites offering free printable coupons for their customers on a daily basis. Visiting these sites can be daunting, so I use the deals websites to see if they are reporting on any good match-ups where a visit to the manufacture website is necessary. Sometimes too, if I see a good deal in my sales flyers, I'll surf around to manufacture websites to see if I can find a deal that wasn't blogged about yet elsewhere.

- **SavingStar:** *eCoupons*
  http://www.savingstar.com
  When I first started loading eCoupons from this site, I didn't realize savings wouldn't be seen at the register. Instead, the site calculates what you have redeemed and offers you a payout each time you reach $5.00. You can cash out earnings toward a PayPal.com payment or an Amazon.com gift card. (There may be more but, as of this writing, this is what I have used.)

Chapter four:

What the Heck Are You Talking About?

"Too many people spend money

they haven't earned,

to buy things they don't want, to

impress people they don't like. "

- Will Smith

These are Catalinas from one shopping trip.

Couponers seem to have their own terminology or "lingo" when discussing their deals. The first time I visited a coupon blog, I had no idea what I was reading because I wasn't up to date on the latest lingo. Here are some common terms (you may encounter more) so you'll know what the heck everyone is talking about:

- **B1G1:** Buy one product, get one for free.
- **B2G1:** Buy two products, get one for free.

- **Catalina:** Catalina coupon that prints the same time your register receipt prints except from a different machine.

- **DND:** Coupon does not double.

- **ECBs:** ExtraCare Bucks through the CVS loyalty rewards program.

- **ETS:** Excludes trial size products.

- **NLA:** the coupon is no longer available.

- **OYNO:** save on your next order.

- **OOP:** how much customers spend out of pocket.

- **OOS:** products are out of stock.

- **Peelie:** Peel-off coupon found on the product's package.

- **Stacking:** Using both a manufacturer's coupon and a store coupon on one item, like at Target for example.

- **Tearpad:** Pad of coupons attached to a display, shelf, or refrigerator door.

- **+UP Reward:** register rewards received through the Rite Aid reward program.

One of the many – MANY – things I love about coupon blogs and websites is how well everything is explained. So, if you come across an abbreviation that is not listed in this mini "lingo" glossary, chances are you will find an explanation somewhere on the site you are visiting. If not, enter "coupon lingo" into your favorite search engine to see if there's another site offering an explanation of the term you are trying to define.

Chapter Five:

Couponing Organizing Tips

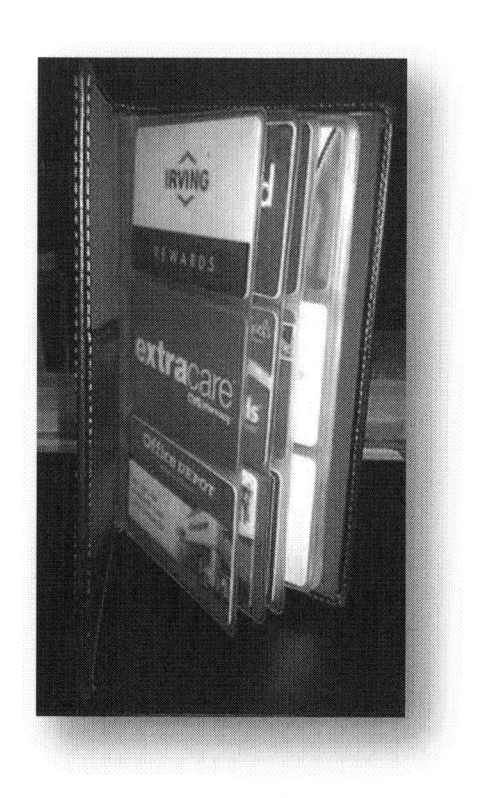

"Act your wage."

- Dave Ramsey

The binder method works best for me.

Now that we've gone over where to get all your coupons and rewards, what do you do with all of this stuff? Everyone has their own way of staying organized so, instead of trying to copy someone else and use a system that doesn't work for you, experiment with numerous methods. I like carrying all of my coupons with me each time I shop so I don't miss out on unadvertised deals, so I use a coupon with plastic inserts to organize my coupons into store sections. There are a couple of other ways of organizing, though, that many couponers love.

File System:

Chrystie V. from the website, I Love to Gossip (http://www.ilovetogossip.com), keeps all her coupons organized in file folders. She uses a filing cabinet and, each time she receives her inserts, she organizes them by type (i.e. Proctor & Gamble, SmartSource, etc.) and by date. Then, she adds each coupon to her database. That way, when a sales rolls around, she can cross reference it with her database, pull the necessary inserts, clip, and compile her grocery lists. She's admitted, though, that the downfall of only carrying coupons that are on her list prevents her from taking advantage of unadvertised deals without making two trips to the store.

Coupon Box:

On the coupon website, Happy Money Saver (http://www.happymoneysaver.com), the site owner uses a plastic latch box, envelopes, and index cards to keep coupons organized. This method allow for portability, so unadvertised deals can be snatched up on the fly. Some boxes are set up with mini file folders, too. This method reminds me a lot of accordion coupon holders, except on a larger scale. Not only can you organize the coupons by type, but you could also set it up so it is organized by store aisle.

The Binder:

As I mentioned above, I prefer the binder method. However, mind is a 2-inch binder that does not zip up because I don't have an enormous cache of coupons. I do have a lot and the little plastic sleeves do become overloaded some months. There are some couponers who prefer those giant zip-up binders (sometimes more than one!) to house their coupon collection. I haven't reached that point yet, but I have come close! I keep mine organized by type of food, but I've given though to organizing it by store aisle so I can grab coupons for unadvertised deals quicker.

*****

Side Note: I also keep all of my rewards cards housed in a business card organizer I found on clearance at Staples. I bought it using a rewards check, so it was FREE. The picture at the beginning of this chapter is what the rewards card holder looks like in use. It's small enough to fit in my purse and portable enough to carry along with my coupon binder.

Chapter Six:

Wait. What About Rain Checks & Rebates?

"It's good to have money and the things that money can buy, but it's good, too, to check up once in a while and make sure that you haven't lost the things that money can't buy."

- *George* Horace *Lorimer*

I keep my receipts for at least one week.

Did you think I was finished sharing ways to save? I'm not! There are additional ways to save at the grocery store! When an item you want to purchase is part of an advertised sale and it is out of stock (OOS), you can request a rain check.

Rain checks must be used within 30 days of the date written on it, and it must be used in the store where it was obtained. Make sure that, when you request the rain check, you are asking for the correct quantity to be written down. You can pick up less than what is written down, but you cannot pick up a larger quantity.

Be sure to check with your grocery store's rain check policy. I've been able to pick up rain checks for products that are part of an unadvertised sale in the past, but my current grocery store no longer offers this deal to its customers. Some grocery stores post their rain check policy right on their websites, whereas others require you to visit their customer service department.

Now, on to rebates . . . I use these for a large number of products, and not just groceries. However, my most recent rebates have involved kitty litter and butter (as shown in the first picture in the beginning of this chapter). However, I love using rebates at stores like Staples so I can pick up free printer paper. I find the most rebates at Staples during the back to school season and am able to cash in on deals for printer paper, pens, pencils, and other supplies.

In addition to checking for unadvertised deals and website promotions, I also look over sales flyers for stores I shop at frequently to see if I can match up a coupon with the rebate offer. For example, I had a coupon for the butter and the kitty litter, so it made the rebate deal even better. Sometimes, when the items go on sale, using coupons and rebates could equal free product.

There are specific terms and conditions for every rebate offer, though, and they differ from each other. For example, sometimes you have to send in the receipt, the rebate peelie from the package, and the UPC code. Other times, you just need to send in a printable form, the cash register receipt, and the UPC code. My favorite scenario is when I can input all the information into an online form and I don't have to mail in anything at all.

Be sure to read the instructions carefully, otherwise you will not receive your rebate. This is frustrating because some offers have many details that must be followed. Pay attention to each of these details and you should be fine.

I've also sent in expired rebates that seemed to be on a package for a long time, like with batteries I bought last year that had an expired offer on them from the previous year. I sent it in anyway, and received a check. The bottom line: keep your receipt in case there are rebate offers inside product packaging!

Chapter Seven:

Knowledge is Power!

Create a Household Binder

"When I was young I thought that money was the most important thing in life; now that I am old I know that it is."

- Oscar Wilde

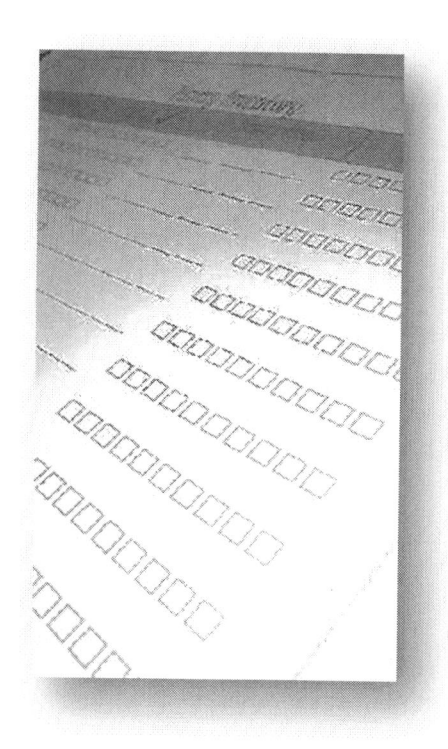

A page from my inventory binder.

Once you start couponing, using rain checks, and cashing in on rebates you are going to notice a stockpile of items growing in your home. Depending on how often you coupon, this stockpile may require a separate storage space. I'll get into that later. First, we're going to discuss how to put all of this couponing knowledge into play. You're going to need a system of organization so you know how much of each product you have, as well as what you are going to need. I have a household binder I keep all of this information in so, when it comes time to compile my shopping list, I have a quick reference guide.

I view household management as a business, so I have a few binders knocking around our home office for various things. So, the binder I'm about to explain is strictly for keeping track of goods while couponing. Yes, that means I have two coupon binders – one for tracking sheets and organization, the other is for my coupons. It may seem like a lot of work, but I've been able to save a ton of money doing things this way. My binder is organized into five sections:

1. Meal Planner
2. Pantry tracking chart
3. Freezer tracking chart
4. Price tracking chart
5. Shopping list

I have these tracking sheets set up so I can take inventory, add inventory after each shopping trip, and update price changes that occur on products I purchase regularly during my regular grocery shopping trips (like milk, bread, and eggs.).

Meal Planner

I set up my meal plans so they are for a three week period of time. That way, I can do a bulk shopping trip for meats, frozen vegetables, and dry goods. Because I plan three weeks out,

I'm able to get a better handle on what I need to keep in my stockpile on a regular basis. This meal planner also prevents me from making purchase I don't need.

Pantry & Freezer Tracking

I take inventory of every single item that is in my pantry (this includes my cupboards in the kitchen and my stockpile), as well as what is in my freezers (my freezer in my kitchen, the extra refrigerator with a freezer on top in our basement, and our chest freezer). I don't take inventory of what is in my refrigerators because these items parish quickly and I know I have to purchase these items weekly.

Price Tracking Chart

Some people believe price hikes occur when sales start, so using a price tracking chart helps alleviate that fear. The chart is also useful for those who shop in multiple stores in order to comparison shop and get the deepest discounts. I use my chart so, when I put together my shopping list, I have a good idea of how much I'll be spending when I reach the register.

Put the Charts to Use!

Once you have created your meal plan and taken inventory of all your products, you are ready to develop the skeleton of your shopping list. Cross-reference your meal plan (write out everything needed for each meal during the planning process) with your inventories and write down what is missing. This is the beginning of your shopping list.

Next, add in perishable items and other items you run out of stock on quickly (like toilet paper, diapers, and so on). This is where you coupons are going to come in. Match up coupons with what you have on your list, and search the Internet to find printable coupons you might be missing. You can do your ad match at the same time so you know which coupons are going to match-up with sales.

Look for FREEBIES!

Even if the items are not on your shopping list or missing from you stockpile, look for freebies. Freebies are items that go on sale and, when adding a coupon or two (if the store allows stacking) or register rewards, they will end up costing nothing out of pocket (OOP). I find freebies every week when I surf around the blogs and websites I frequent so I can add to my stockpile.

I scanned pages from my tracking binder and shared them with you in the appendix at the back of this book.

Chapter Seven:

What is the Purpose of a Stockpile?

"After a certain point, money is meaningless. It ceases to be the goal. The game is what counts."

- Aristotle Onassis

This case of toilet paper was FREE thanks to SwagBucks.com!

Just like everyone has their own reasons for using coupons, everyone also has their own reason for stockpiling. Like I mentioned in the beginning of this book, my husband and I are both self-employed. There are months when our income is fine and we have plenty of funds coming in to cover our bills. When there is a surplus, I hide that money away for when business starts falling off. For each of us, there are at least three months out of every year for each of our businesses where this fund has come in handy. The thing about this fund, though, is I don't like using it for food or household items.

So, with that in mind, I started stockpiling. We have no idea if prices are going to continue skyrocketing with each passing month, and we have no idea where the economy is going to head. When I first started couponing and stockpiling, no one was doing well financially (in our close circle of friends and family), so I wanted to have more than one safety net in place. Our stockpile allows us to take comfort in knowing we can feed our family for at least one month if our income becomes a challenge.

My stockpile contains:

- Cereal and other storable breakfast items
- Canned goods
- Salad dressings
- Spaghetti sauce
- Other types of sauces
- Rice and other side dishes
- Pasta and noodles
- Baking mixes and desserts
- Coffee and creamer
- Health and beauty items
- Cleaning supplies
- Pet supplies
- Beverages
- Frozen meats
- Frozen vegetables
- Frozen dinners
- Paper goods

- Canning supplies

There is no right or wrong way to set up a stockpile. Mine is set up using an old cabinet we didn't have use for in the main part of our home anymore. My plan is to get rid of this thing and utilize shelving instead. Because my space is limited, my system of organization is not what I would call useful. However, when shelving is put in its place, I'll be able to group things together in a more efficient (for me) way.

Most couponing websites and blogs have pictures of stockpiles for others to use as a guide. I also belong to several coupon groups on Facebook.com where pictures of stockpiles are frequently posted. This gives me ideas for how to organize my stockpile, as well as what offers and deals I should be on the lookout for based upon what is in their stock. Remember, the Internet is an excellent tool for couponing, organizing, and efficiency.

Chapter Eight:

How Else Can We Save More Money?

"There are people who have money and people who are rich."

- Coco Chanel

Pinching every penny counts in a "down" economy.

Even after I've saved a ton of money on groceries, I still look for additional ways to save on our everyday household expenses. Couponing has allowed us to afford many things we typically couldn't enjoy in the past – like going to the movies once per month or eating out with the kids. However, I still want to get our bills even lower.

The first thing I did was make a list of all our regular bills and their monthly payments. There are several bills that I'm not able to lower right now, like loan payments, memberships, and the cost of our Internet connection, so I place those items in my "static" list because they don't change often. In my "I can lower this list," I include:

- Electric bill
- Cell phone bills
- Heating bills
- Satellite bill
- Gas
- Insurance policies

There is a program through my home state, Maine, which helps lower the cost of electricity use for every resident. It is called Electricity Maine (http://www.electricityme.com) and, when residents sign up, they will see their electric bills lower starting around two or three months following the sign-up month. The percentage isn't huge, but it's enough to make a difference. I highly recommend that you check with your state to see if there are opportunities to save on your electric bill.

We've been able to reduce our cell phone bills simply by going into our cell phone carrier location and saying, "is there a better deal we could be getting?" We've done this twice and have been able to get a better monthly deal. This doesn't always happen because we have a contract agreement, but it doesn't hurt to ask.

Okay, heating bills is a challenge here because we live in a wintery state. We've been able to lower the cost of heating by using a pellet stove as our primary heat source and using our oil furnace as a secondary source. When we run into issues with paying for oil, we have used Joe-4-Oil (Citizens Energy - http://www.citizensenergy.com/main/Home.html) in the past. We're also going to start using a wood stove and heat using trees we've cut from our property.

Our satellite bill is another one we've been able to reduce twice since we started using this service in 2006. The company we use offers different package deals for cheaper prices, so we've switched twice to reduce our bill. There are also earning opportunities when we refer new customers to the service. We've been able to take advantage of that opportunity three times so far.

Saving on gas is a challenge, especially when gas prices continue to rise on a regular basis. We've kept up on the maintenance on our vehicles, including tire maintenance, which shows improvement with gas mileage. We also plan our trips better (everything we do is out of town, unfortunately, because we live in the middle of nowhere) so we are using less gas. In addition to these tricks, we also use reward cards from every gas station that offers them. The savings we've experienced from doing these simple things has been noticeable.

Insurance policies are another area where I've been able to find savings. For example, we group together our vehicle policies with our home owner's insurance so we can get a discount. There are also discounts for paperless billing, automatic payments, having non-smokers in the house, and paying premiums on time. Our insurance policies see a decrease yearly based upon those few changes. I also call every six months to see if there are opportunities for additional savings. I was calling more often than that, but I've noticed it's about every six months with my insurance carrier when I see discounts applied. It doesn't hurt to ask!

Conclusion

Are You Ready to Start Saving?

*"A man who both spends

and saves money is

the happiest man,

because he has both enjoyments."*

- Samuel Johnson

I look for ways to cut my budget every week.

I had a couple of goals when writing this book. The first was to give novices a clearer understanding of what the wonderful world of couponing is all about. The second was to share my story, my strategies, and my money-saving methods. I didn't want to bog readers down with too much information, or too many resources because that can be overwhelming in a matter of minutes.

Instead, I've decided to keep this resources short, sweet, and to the point. I'm thinking about developing a companion workbook to go along with this guide, as well as some other money-saving tip books that delve deeper into saving for college, IRAs, estate planning, homesteading, and other financial aspects of life we all must touch upon at one time or another. Until then, I hope this book is helpful in your money-saving endeavors!

Resources:

Resource Links I've Used Along the Way

1. http://www.ilovetogossip.com
2. http://www.thetheivingbear.com
3. http://www.mavenofsavin.com
4. http://www.happymoneysaver.com
5. http://www.swagbucks.com
6. http://www.savingstar.com
7. http://www.redplum.com
8. http://www.smartsource.com
9. http://www.couponnetwork.com
10. http://www.couponsthingsbydede.com
11. http://www.electricityme.com
12. http://www.citizensenergy.com/main/Home.html

Appendix A:

Shopping List

Appendix B:

Price Tracking Chart

Price Tracking Chart

Item: _____

Date:	Store:	Price:	Unit Price:

Appendix C:

Meal Planner

Meal Planner: 3 Weeks

Date	Week 1	Date	Week 2	Date	Week 3
SUNDAY __/__	Breakfast. Lunch. Dinner.	SUNDAY __/__	Breakfast. Lunch. Dinner.	SUNDAY __/__	Breakfast. Lunch. Dinner.
MONDAY __/__	Breakfast. Lunch. Dinner.	MONDAY __/__	Breakfast. Lunch. Dinner.	MONDAY __/__	Breakfast. Lunch. Dinner.
TUESDAY __/__	Breakfast. Lunch. Dinner.	TUESDAY __/__	Breakfast. Lunch. Dinner.	TUESDAY __/__	Breakfast. Lunch. Dinner.
WEDNESDAY __/__	Breakfast. Lunch. Dinner.	WEDNESDAY __/__	Breakfast. Lunch. Dinner.	WEDNESDAY __/__	Breakfast. Lunch. Dinner.
THURSDAY __/__	Breakfast. Lunch. Dinner.	THURSDAY __/__	Breakfast. Lunch. Dinner.	THURSDAY __/__	Breakfast. Lunch. Dinner.
FRIDAY __/__	Breakfast. Lunch. Dinner.	FRIDAY __/__	Breakfast. Lunch. Dinner.	FRIDAY __/__	Breakfast. Lunch. Dinner.
SATURDAY __/__	Breakfast. Lunch. Dinner.	SATURDAY __/__	Breakfast. Lunch. Dinner.	SATURDAY __/__	Breakfast. Lunch. Dinner.

Appendix D:

Pantry Inventory

Description	In Stock ✓	Description	In Stock ✓
_____	☐☐☐☐☐☐☐☐☐	_____	☐☐☐☐☐☐☐☐☐
_____	☐☐☐☐☐☐☐☐☐	_____	☐☐☐☐☐☐☐☐☐
_____	☐☐☐☐☐☐☐☐☐	_____	☐☐☐☐☐☐☐☐☐
_____	☐☐☐☐☐☐☐☐☐	_____	☐☐☐☐☐☐☐☐☐
_____	☐☐☐☐☐☐☐☐☐	_____	☐☐☐☐☐☐☐☐☐
_____	☐☐☐☐☐☐☐☐☐	_____	☐☐☐☐☐☐☐☐☐
_____	☐☐☐☐☐☐☐☐☐	_____	☐☐☐☐☐☐☐☐☐
_____	☐☐☐☐☐☐☐☐☐	_____	☐☐☐☐☐☐☐☐☐
_____	☐☐☐☐☐☐☐☐☐	_____	☐☐☐☐☐☐☐☐☐
_____	☐☐☐☐☐☐☐☐☐	_____	☐☐☐☐☐☐☐☐☐
_____	☐☐☐☐☐☐☐☐☐	_____	☐☐☐☐☐☐☐☐☐
_____	☐☐☐☐☐☐☐☐☐	_____	☐☐☐☐☐☐☐☐☐
_____	☐☐☐☐☐☐☐☐☐	_____	☐☐☐☐☐☐☐☐☐
_____	☐☐☐☐☐☐☐☐☐	_____	☐☐☐☐☐☐☐☐☐
_____	☐☐☐☐☐☐☐☐☐	_____	☐☐☐☐☐☐☐☐☐
_____	☐☐☐☐☐☐☐☐☐	_____	☐☐☐☐☐☐☐☐☐
_____	☐☐☐☐☐☐☐☐☐	_____	☐☐☐☐☐☐☐☐☐
_____	☐☐☐☐☐☐☐☐☐	_____	☐☐☐☐☐☐☐☐☐

Appendix E:

Freezer Inventory

Description	In Stock ✓	Description	In Stock ✓
_____	☐☐☐☐☐☐☐☐☐	_____	☐☐☐☐☐☐☐☐☐
_____	☐☐☐☐☐☐☐☐☐	_____	☐☐☐☐☐☐☐☐☐
_____	☐☐☐☐☐☐☐☐☐	_____	☐☐☐☐☐☐☐☐☐
_____	☐☐☐☐☐☐☐☐☐	_____	☐☐☐☐☐☐☐☐☐
_____	☐☐☐☐☐☐☐☐☐	_____	☐☐☐☐☐☐☐☐☐
_____	☐☐☐☐☐☐☐☐☐	_____	☐☐☐☐☐☐☐☐☐
_____	☐☐☐☐☐☐☐☐☐	_____	☐☐☐☐☐☐☐☐☐
_____	☐☐☐☐☐☐☐☐☐	_____	☐☐☐☐☐☐☐☐☐
_____	☐☐☐☐☐☐☐☐☐	_____	☐☐☐☐☐☐☐☐☐
_____	☐☐☐☐☐☐☐☐☐	_____	☐☐☐☐☐☐☐☐☐
_____	☐☐☐☐☐☐☐☐☐	_____	☐☐☐☐☐☐☐☐☐
_____	☐☐☐☐☐☐☐☐☐	_____	☐☐☐☐☐☐☐☐☐
_____	☐☐☐☐☐☐☐☐☐	_____	☐☐☐☐☐☐☐☐☐
_____	☐☐☐☐☐☐☐☐☐	_____	☐☐☐☐☐☐☐☐☐
_____	☐☐☐☐☐☐☐☐☐	_____	☐☐☐☐☐☐☐☐☐
_____	☐☐☐☐☐☐☐☐☐	_____	☐☐☐☐☐☐☐☐☐
_____	☐☐☐☐☐☐☐☐☐	_____	☐☐☐☐☐☐☐☐☐
_____	☐☐☐☐☐☐☐☐☐	_____	☐☐☐☐☐☐☐☐☐
_____	☐☐☐☐☐☐☐☐☐	_____	☐☐☐☐☐☐☐☐☐

About the Author

Jennifer Greenleaf is a mother of two boys, ages eleven and thirteen, and a stepmother to one daughter age twelve. She and her husband blended their family in 2004 when the kids were two, three, and four years of age.

During their money-saving journey they have gardened, raised chickens for their eggs, raised two pigs. She is also growing an orange tree, despite the freezing cold temperatures in Maine, and the entire family is downsizing from a sprawling range into a cottage sized Cape Cod style home sometime during 2013. Following the move, Jennifer intends to start a local coupon swap.

Jennifer Greenleaf has been a freelance writer since 1999 and an author since 2006. She enjoys writing informative how-to style non-fiction articles and books, but she is also working on several fiction manuscripts as well. She hopes to have her first novel released by the end of 2013. You can learn more about Jennifer on her website, http://www.jennifergreenleaf.com and her mothering adventures on http://www.mainelymotherhood.info. Her books are all available on Amazon.com right now and, in the future, will be available through Barnes & Noble.